Introduction

OXFORD, 'that sweet City with her dreaming spires', is a jewel in our heritage. Since AD 1200 it has been the home of Britain's oldest University, and in eight centuries the founding of many colleges has made Oxford a unique city of fine buildings. This great inheritance is here to be seen, and this little book will show the way.

Introduction

Oxford, 'cette cit… mante aux flèche… est un des joyau… patrimoine anglais. La création de l'université, la plus ancienne d'Angleterre, remonte à l'an 1200. Pendant huit siècles, de nombreux collèges se sont établis dans des bâtiments magnifiques qui font d'Oxford une cité unique. Ce petit guide se propose de vous en montrer la route.

…, ist ein Kleinod in unserem kulturellen Erbe. Die älteste Universität Großbritanniens entstand hier um 1200, und im Laufe von achthundert Jahren hat die Gründung vieler Colleges Oxford zu einer architektonisch einzigartigen Stadt gemacht. Besucher können diese große Tradition hier betrachten.

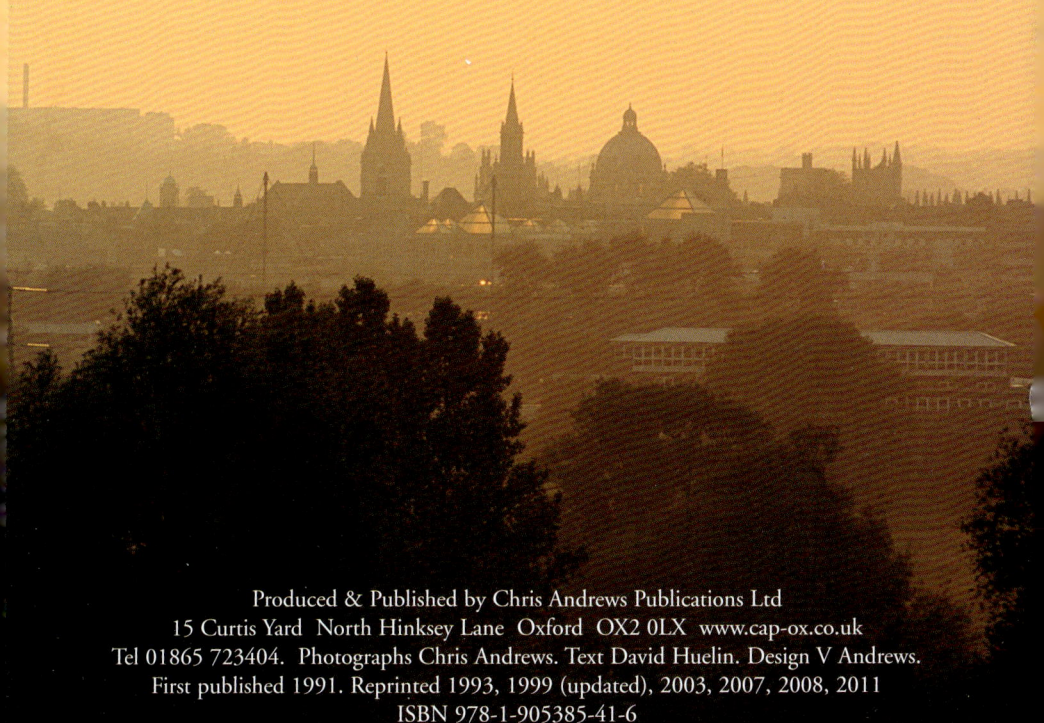

Produced & Published by Chris Andrews Publications Ltd
15 Curtis Yard North Hinksey Lane Oxford OX2 0LX www.cap-ox.co.uk
Tel 01865 723404. Photographs Chris Andrews. Text David Huelin. Design V Andrews.
First published 1991. Reprinted 1993, 1999 (updated), 2003, 2007, 2008, 2011
ISBN 978-1-905385-41-6

University Buildings

The Bodleian Library

Bodleian Library - 1598 - Old Schools Quad, Broad Street, and Radcliffe Square - map ref 3E

World's largest academic library; 6 million books, 1 million maps. Old Schools Quadrangle, 1619, contains lecture halls of the medieval 'schools' or faculties, names above the doors.

La plus grande bibliothèque universitaire au monde: 6 millions de volumes, un million de cartes géographiques. Le Old Schools Quadrangle, 1619, abrite les salles des 'écoles' ou facultés médiévales, dont les noms se trouvent au dessus des portes.

Größte akademische Bibliothek der Welt; sechs Millionen Bücher und eine Million Karten. Innenhof der alten Schulen, 1619, über den Türen die Namen der mittelalterlichen Fakultäten.

Clarendon Building - 1713 - Broad Street - map ref 3E

University offices and Proctors' headquarters.

Services administratifs de l'université et bureau central des censeurs

Universitätsverwaltung und Sitz der 'Proctors.'

Radcliffe Camera - 1749 - Radcliffe Square - map ref 3E see pic p29.

Built for the books given to the University by Dr John Radcliffe. Now the principal reading room of the Bodleian Library.

Construit pour abriter les livres légués à l'université par le Dr John Radcliffe. Utilisé aujourd'hui comme salle de lecture principale de la Bodleian Library.

Erbaut für Werke, die der Universität von Dr John Radcliffe hinterlassen wurden. Heute der Hauptlesesaal der Bodleian.

University Buildings

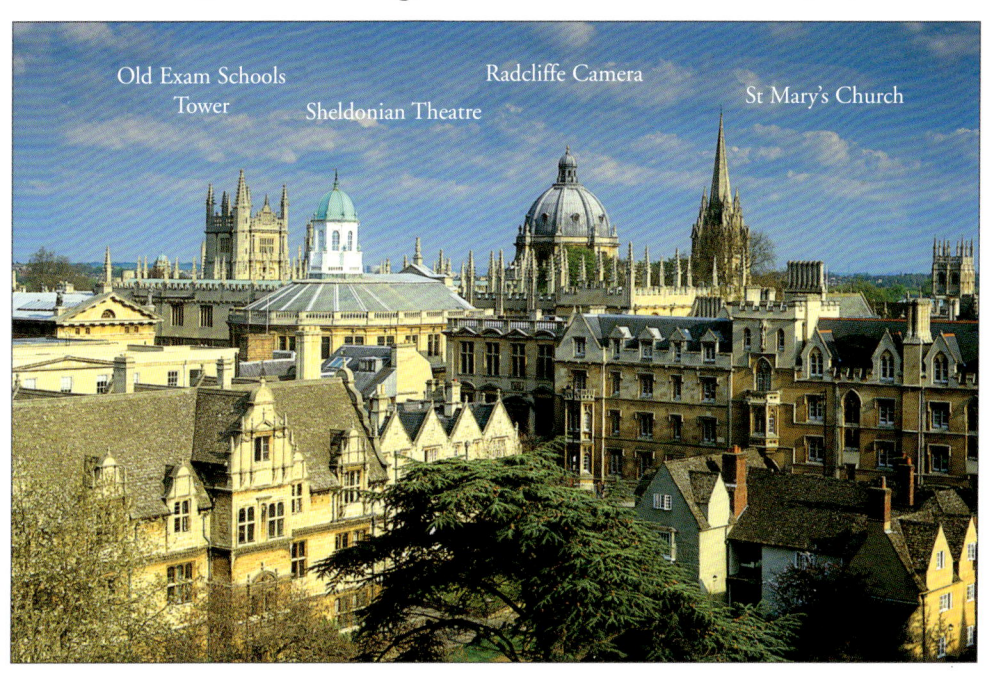

Oxford from the north

Old Exam Schools Tower
Sheldonian Theatre
Radcliffe Camera
St Mary's Church

Sheldonian Theatre - 1669 - Broad Street - map ref 3E

Designed by Christopher Wren as an assembly hall for degree-giving and other ceremonials; also used for concerts.

Conçu par Christopher Wren comme salle de remise des diplômes et autres manifestations officielles, il sert aussi de salle de concerts.

Errichtet nach den Plänen des Architekten Christopher Wren als Versammlungsort für Universitätszeremonien wie z.B. die Verleihung akademischer Grade. Außerdem genutzt als Konzertsaal.

St Mary the Virgin, University Church - 1280 - High Street - map ref 3E

Before the Sheldonian was built, St Mary's was used for university business of all kinds, some of it too rowdy for a church.

Avant la construction du Sheldonian Theatre St Mary était utilisée pour toutes sortes d'activités de l'université, dont certaines étaient trop tapageuses pour se tenir dans une église.

Vor der Errichtung des Sheldonian Theaters wurde St Mary's für alle möglichen Angelegenheiten der Universität genutzt, von denen manche für eine Kirche ungeeignet waren.

Examination Schools - 1882 - High Street - 4E

The new Schools building of lecture halls was put up to meet growing needs, and to allow the Bodleian to use the vacated space in the Old Schools.

Ces nouvelles salles ont été construites pour faire face aux besoins croissants de l'université et pour permettre à la Bodleian Library d'utiliser l'espace ainsi laissé vacant dans les Old Schools.

Der zunehmende Raumbedarf und der Wunsch der Bodleian nach neuen Stellplätzen für Bücher führten Ende des 19 Jahrhunderts zur Errichtung des neuen 'Schools' Gebäudes.

All Souls College High Street   3/4E

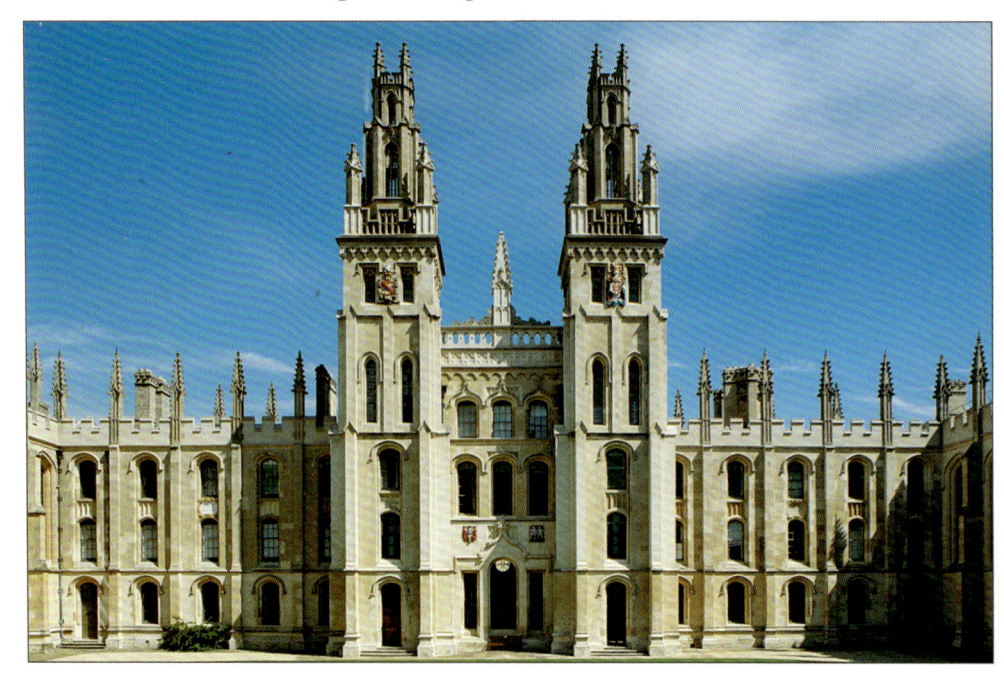

Founded
1438 Archbishop Henry Chichele as the College of All Souls of The Faithful Departed

Buildings
Front Quad, Chapel, 1440s; North Quad, Hall, Codrington Library, 1730s by Nicholas Hawksmoor and Warden Dr Clarke.

Past Members
Archbp. Gilbert Sheldon; Sir Christopher Wren; T.E. Lawrence (of Arabia)

Note
Ninth oldest college. Founded to pray for all the souls of men who had died in the wars against France; later became a select club for distinguished graduates only. Once every hundred years the Warden and Fellows process by night with flaming torches through the college ritually searching for a mallard (wild duck) and singing a 17th-century song.

Neuvième collège établi à Oxford. Fondé pour prier pour le salut des âmes des hommes morts pendant les guerres contre la France, il devint par la suite un cercle d'élite réservé aux licenciés éminents. Tous les 100 ans, le directeur et les autres membres forment une procession rituelle, avançant dans la nuit avec des torches à la recherche d'un canard sauvage tout en chantant un air du dix-septième siècle.

Gegründet zum Gedenken an die Seelen all der Männer, die in den Kriegen gegen Frankreich gefallen waren. Später wurde es zu einer exklusiven Gemeinschaft, die nur herausragende Akademiker und diese allein zum Zwecke der Forschung aufnimmt. Alle hundert Jahre ziehen einem alten Ritus gemäß 'Warden' und die 'Fellows' in einem nächtlichen Fackelzug durch die Gebäude und suchen eine Wildente, wobei sie einen Gesang aus dem 17. Jahrhundert zu Gehör bringen.

Balliol College Broad Street   2/3 D/E

Founded
1263 John de Balliol and his wife Princess Dervorguilla.

Buildings
Library (Front Quad) 15th century. Chapel and other buildings 19th-20th century.

Past Members
Harold Macmillan (Lord Stockton, Chancellor 1960-86); Graham Greene; Roy Jenkins (Lord Jenkins, Chancellor 1986-2002).

Note
One of the three oldest colleges. Founded as a penance when John de Balliol quarrelled with the Bishop of Durham and was defeated. College prominent in 19th century when Balliol men had a reputation for effortless superiority. Ancient gates (in passage to Garden Quad) scorched by fire of Martyrs burned at the stake outside, 1555-6.

L'un des trois collèges les plus anciens.
A la suite d'une querelle avec l'évêque de Durham, John de Balliol dut, en réparation, construire ce collège. Collège important au dix-neuvième quand les hommes de Balliol avaient la réputation d'une 'supériorité sans effort'. Les portes anciennes (dans le passage du Garden Quad) sont roussies par les flammes des martyres brûlés sur les bûchers, 1555/6.

Eines der drei ältesten Colleges. Seine Gründung war die Bußtat John de Balliols, der im Streit mit dem Bischof von Durham unterlegen war. Im 19 Jahrhundert ragte dieses College besonders heraus, als man seinen Mitgliedern 'mühelose Überlegenheit' nachsagte. Das alte Eingangstor (im Durchgang zum 'Garden Quad') ist noch vom Feuer des Scheiterhaufens gezeichnet, auf dem man in den Jahren 1555 und 1556 Märtyrer verbrannte.

Brasenose College Radcliffe Square 3E

Founded
1509 Bishop William Smyth and Sir Richard Sutton, of Lancashire.

Buildings
Old Quad and hall 1509-16 chapel 1666; New Quad 1909 (Thomas Jackson).

Past Members
Dr George Clarke (All Souls); Earl Haig (Field Marshal); John Buchan; Robert Runcie (Archbp.); Michael Palin.

Note
Built on the site of Brazen Nose Hall, which had on its gate a bronze knocker or sanctuary ring in the form of an animal snout. In the riots of 1334 scholars fled to Stamford (Lincolnshire) taking the nose with them. The college got it back only in 1890; it is now in the dining hall. A visitor in 1617 was John Middleton, 9ft tall.

Construit sur le terrain de Brazen Nose Hall, qui tenait sur sa porte d'entrée un heurtoir ou anneau en bronze représentant le groin d'un animal. Pendant les émeutes de 1334, les étudiants s'enfuirent à Stamford (Lincolnshire) en emportant le heurtoir avec eux. Il ne fut rendu au collège qu'en 1890 et se trouve aujourd'hui dans le réfectoire. La légende dit que John Middleton, qui visita le collège en 1617, mesurait 2,75m.

Auf dem Gelände von Brazen Nose Hall errichtet, deren Tor ein bronzener Türklopfer oder ein Ring in der Form einer Tierschnauze oder -nase zierte. Während der Unruhen des Jahres 1334 nahmen Gelehrte auf ihrer Flucht nach Stamford (Lincolnshire) jene Nase mit. Erst 1890 kam sie wieder in den Besitz des Colleges. Sie befindet sich nun im Speisesaal. Ein gewisser John Middleton war 1617 Gast des Colleges, ein Hüne von über zweieinhalb Metern Körpergröße, dessen Hände allein fast einen halben Meter germessen haben sollen.

Christ Church - Cathedral and House   3F

Founded
Cathedral 1120, is also chapel of college founded 1525 by Cardinal Wolsey, refounded 1546 by Henry VIII.

Buildings
Chapter House 13th century. Hall, gatehouse, part of Great Quad 1520s; rest of Quad 1660s. Tom Tower (by Wren) 1682; Peckwater Quad, Library, Canterbury Gate and Quad, 18th century.

Past Members
William Penn (founder Pennsylvania USA); C.L. Dodgson (Lewis Carroll);Edward VII (when Prince of Wales); fourteen Prime Ministers.

Note
The largest of Oxford's colleges combined with the smallest cathedral in England. Magnificent architecture and grounds, including a fountain and picture gallery. Bowler-hatted custodians still patrol there. Lewis Carroll's 'Alice' was the daughter of the Dean, Henry Liddell.

Christ Church est le plus grand collège d'Oxford et il abrite la plus petite cathédrale d'Angleterre. Les bâtiments et les terrains magnifiques comprennent une fontaine et une galerie de tableaux. Les gardiens y portent toujours le chapeau melon. C'est la fille du doyen Henry Liddell qui inspira l'Alice' de Lewis Carroll.

Das größte der Oxforder Colleges - zugleich die kleinste von Englands Kathedralen. Eindrucksvolle Architektur und hochinteressante Anlagen. Unter anderem findet man einen hübschen Brunnen und eine sehr sehenswerte Bildergalerie. Noch immer machen hier Wächter in

Melonen die Runder. Die kleine 'Alice' aus Lewis Carrolls weltberühmten Kinderbüchern war die Tochter des ehemaligen Deans Henry Liddell.

Corpus Christi College Merton Street   3F

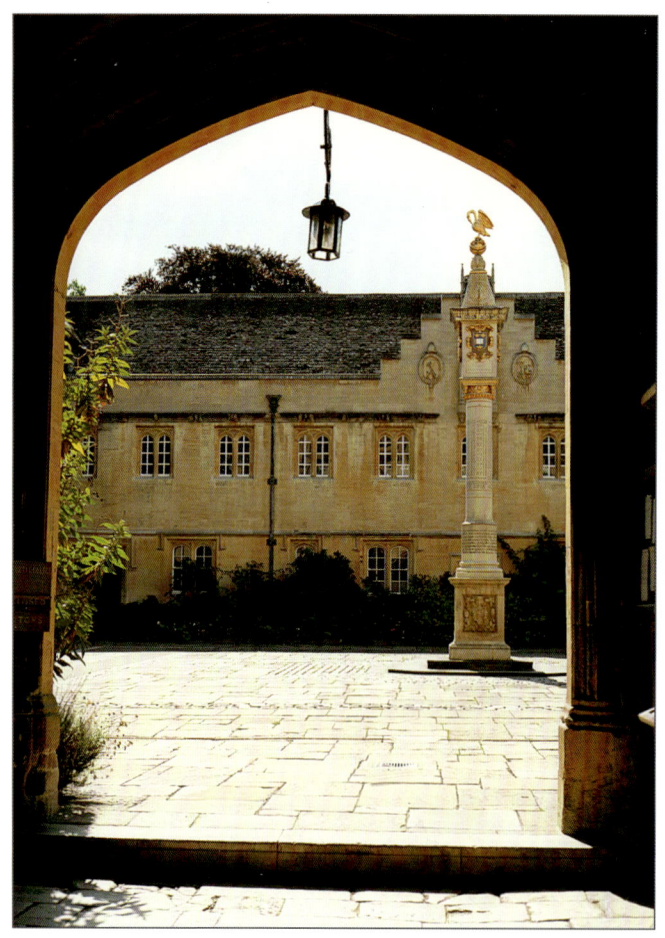

of arms; it is a symbol of the Body of Christ and gives the college its name. Corpus had Oxford's first professor of Greek among its Fellows, and is still academically eminent. Also the home of the annual tortoise racing.

Corpus Chrisi est le plus petit des collèges pour étudiants de premier cycle, mais non des moins importants. Le pélican (réplique moderne) provient du blason de l'évêque Fox: c'est un symbole du corps du Christ et il a donné son nom au collège. Corpus fut le premier des collèges d'Oxford à avoir un professeur de Grec parmi ses membres. Il accueille par ailleurs une course annuelle de tortues

Corpus ist das kleinste, wohl kaum aber das unbedeutendste der Oxforder Colleges, die Studienanfänger aufnehmen. Der Pelikan (Kopie) stammt aus dem Wappen des Bischofs Fox. Er ist ein Symbol für den Leib Christi und gibt dem College seinen Namen. Oxfords erster Professor für Altgriechisch ist Mitglied dieses Colleges. Zudem findet hier ein jährliches Schildkrötenrennen statt.

Founded
1517 Bishop Richard Fox, Lord Privy Seal to Henry VIII, Chancellor Cambridge University.

Buildings
Front Quad, hall and chapel 1517, refaced 1937. Column with pelican 1581; Fellows' Building 1712, Dean Aldrich.

Past Members
General Oglethorpe (founder, Georgia); John Keble, Thomas Arnold.

Note
Corpus is the smallest of the undergraduate colleges, but not the least important. The pelican (modern replica) comes from Bishop Fox's coat

Exeter College Turl Street   3E

Founded
1314 Walter Stapledon,
Bishop of Exeter

Buildings
Front Quad 1672-1703
Palmer's Tower 1432.
Chapel 1860.

Past Members
Edward Burne-Jones; William Morris; J.R.R. Tolkien; Nevill Coghill, Alan Bennet.

Note
The fourth oldest college. Front quad has dining hall of 1618 with fine original roof and screen; Victorian French Gothic chapel with tapestry by Edward Burne-Jones and William Morris, *The Adoration of the Magi.*

Doorway 5 leads to Fellows' Garden, where from the embankment there is a good view of the Radcliffe Camera.

Quatrième collège établi a Oxford.
Le Front Quad abrite le réfectoire qui date de 1618, au toit splendide et au paravant d'origine. La chapelle est dans le style gothique français; elle abrite une tapisserie de Edward Burne-Jones et William Morris *(Adoration des Mages)*. La porte numéro 5 permet de se rendre au jardin, d'où l'on a une très belle vue sur la Radcliffe Camera.

Der Speisesaal im 'Front Quad' (vorderer Innenhof) stammt aus dem Jahre 1618 und zeigt noch heute die Originaldecke und Trennwand am Eingang. Kapelle im Stil viktorianischer Imitation der französischen Gotik mit Wandteppichen von Edward Burne-Jones und William Morris, *Die Anbetung der Könige*. Eingang 5 führt zum Fellow-Garten, von dessen östlicher Ummauerung man einen schönen Blick auf die Radcliffe Camera hat.

11

Hertford College Catte Street 3E

Founded
1283 Hart Hall
1740 Hertford College
1822 Magdalen Hall
1874 Hertford College

Buildings
Catte Street front 1822; library, 1716; Front Quad, hall stair-tower, chapel, 1880s-1900s; Bridge of Sighs 1914; all by Thomas Jackson.

Past Members
John Donne; Edward Hyde (Earl Clarendon); Jonathan (Dean) Swift; Evelyn Waugh.

Note
Hertford College began as Hart Hall in the 1280's. It was acquired by Walter de Stapledon, Bishop of Exeter, for a community of scholars, and named Stapledon Hall. In 1740 it was refounded as Hertford College, but it was not successful and it was closed in 1818. Hart Hall was refounded for the fourth time in 1874 by the banker Thomas Baring and renamed Hertford College.

Au début, dans les années 1280, Hertford College s'appelait Hart Hall. Il fut acquis par Walter de Stapledon, évêque d'Exeter, pour une communauté de lettrés, et nommé Stapledon Hall, En 1740 il fut refondé sous le nom de Hertford College, mais sans succès, et il fut fermé en 1818. Hart Hall fut refondé pour la quatrième fois en 1874 par le banquier Thomas Baring et rebaptisé Hertford College.

Hertford College wurde in den 1280er Jahren als Hart Hall gegründet. Es wurde von Walter de Stapledon, Bischoff von Exeter, für eine Gelehrtengemeinde erworben, und den Namen Stapledon Hall gegeben. 1740 wurde es als Hertford College wiedergegründet; aber ohne Erfolg. Es wurde also im Jahre 1818 geschlossen. Im Jahre 1874 wurde Hart Hall zum vierten mal vom Bankier Thomas Baring geöffnet und den Namen Hertford College gegeben.

Jesus College Turl Street　　　　　　　　　　2/3E

Founded
1571 Hugh Price with help from Queen Elizabeth I.

Buildings
Front Quad, chapel and hall 16th-17th century. Second Quad 1640s onwards. An opening in the north range leads to the buildings on Ship Street, 1905, and to the Old Members' Building, 1971.

Past Members
Richard 'Beau' Nash; T.E. Lawrence (of Arabia); Harold Wilson; Magnus Magnussen.

Note
College was intended primarily for scholars from Wales, and the Welsh connection remains strong. Small peaceful quads with flowering borders; domestic atmosphere. Chapel has bust of T.E. Lawrence. First men's college to admit women, in 1974.

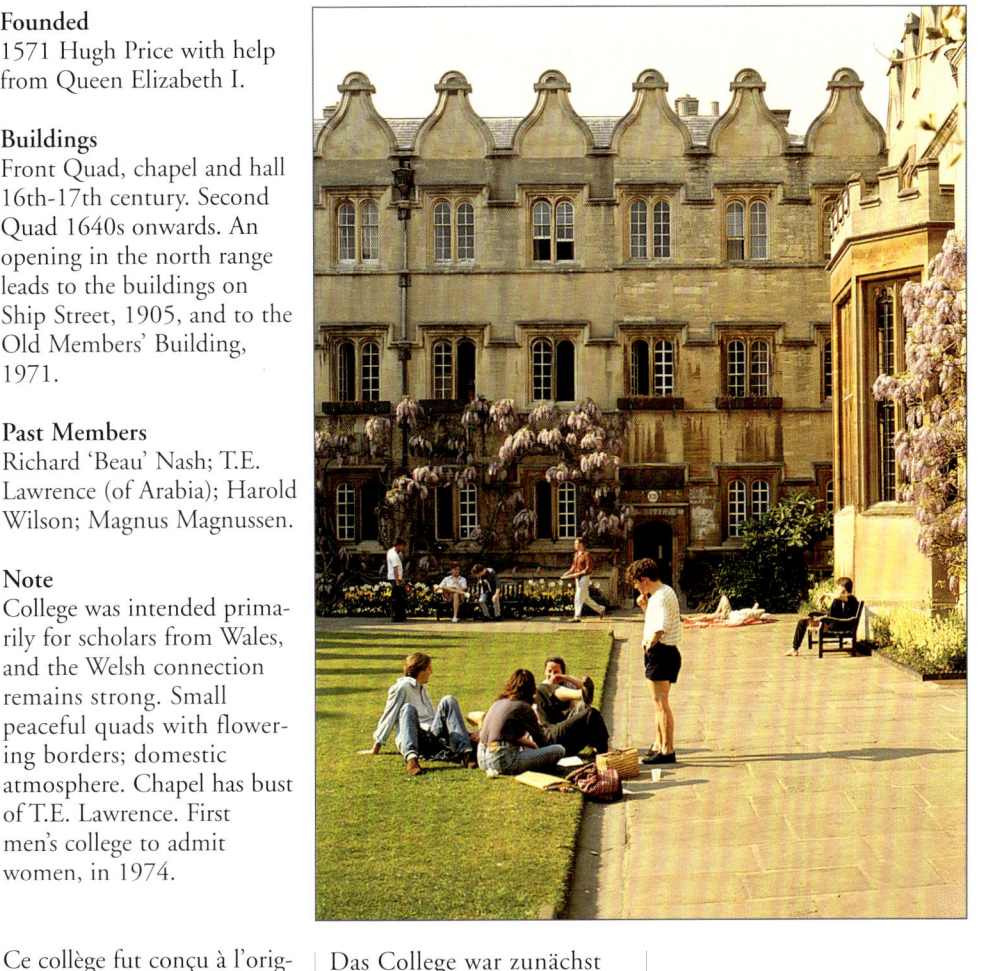

Ce collège fut conçu à l'origine pour les lettrés du Pays de Galles, et cette connection reste importante. L'atmosphère y est conviviale; les petites cours, calmes et tranquilles, sont bordées de fleurs. La chapelle renferme un buste de T.E. Lawrence. Jesus College fut le premier collège d'hommes à admettre les femmes, en 1974.

Das College war zunächst hauptsächlich für Waliser bestimmt, und die Verbindungen zu Wales sind immer stark. Friedliche kleine Quads mit schönen Blumenbeeten. Häusliche Atmosphäre. In der Kapelle eine Büste von T.E. Lawrence, Ließ als erstes Männercollege 1974 Frauen zu.

Lincoln College Turl Street 3E

Founded
1427 Richard Fleming and 1479 Thomas Rotherham, both Bishops of Lincoln.

Buildings
Front Quad 15th century, Chapel and Chapel Quad early 17th century. Library: All Saints Church 1708.

Past Members
William Davenant (Shakespeare's godson); Dr John Radcliffe; John Wesley; Osbert Lancaster; John Le Carré.

Note
Eighth oldest college. Bishop Fleming wanted young priests to be taught to 'defend the mysteries of Scripture'.

John Wesley was a Fellow in the 1730s and held meetings of the 'Holy Club' in his room. Attractive college with fine library in converted All Saints Church.

Huitième collège établi à Oxford.
L'Evêque Fleming voulait que l'on enseigne aux jeunes prêtres à défendre les mystères des Ecritures Saintes. John Wesley a été membre du collège vers 1730 et tenait les réunions du 'Holy Club' dans sa chambre. Lincoln est un beau collège où l'église de All Saints a été convertie en une très belle bibliothèque.

Achtältestes College.
Bischof Fleming wünschte, daß junge Priester hier in der 'Verteidigung der Mysterien der hl. Schrift' unterrichtet würden. In der 30er Jahren des 18. Jahrhundert war John Welsey ein Fellow dieses Colleges und versammelte die 'Heilige Gesellschaft' (Holy Club) regelmäßig in seinem Zimmer.

Magdalen College High Street   4/5E

Founded
1458 William of Wayneflete

Buildings
Front Quad (St John's), Chapel, gatehouse, hall and central cloister 1470s to 1480s. Bell Tower 1492-1509. Old Grammar Hall 1614. New Buildings, 1733, 1999.

Past Members
Cardinal Wolsey; Oscar Wilde; C.S. Lewis; Prince of Wales (Edward VIII); Lord Denning; Dudley Moore.

Note
Tenth oldest college.

Famous Bell Tower is one of Oxford's finest buildings; at dawn on May Day the college choir goes to the top and sings to the crowds below. College grounds 40 hectares of riverside walks, deer park and gardens. Buildings with many gargoyles, grotesque figures and portraits of Fellows and Bursars.

Dixième collège établi à Oxford.

Le célèbre beffroi est l'un des plus beaux bâtiments d'Oxford. Au point du jour, le premier mai, le choeur du collège monte au sommet et chante pour la foule assemblée en bas. Les terres du collège s'étendent sur 40 hectares, permettant de belles promenades le long de la rivière, dans le parc aux cerfs et dans les jardins. Les bâtisses du collège sont ornées de nombreuses gargouilles et de figures grotesques.

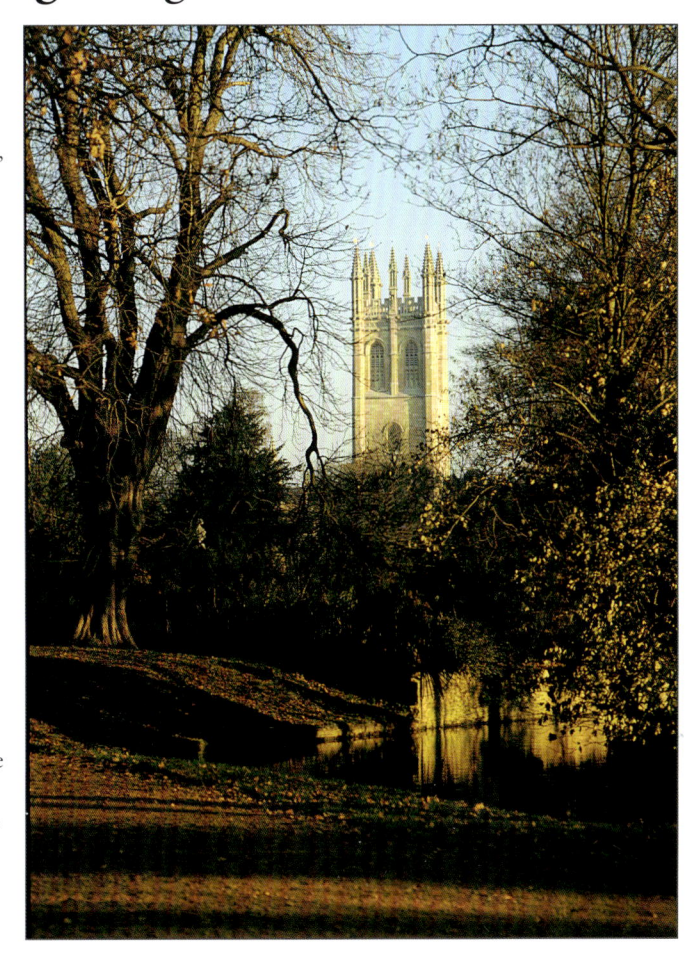

Zehntältestes College.

Der berühmte Glockenturm ist einer von Oxfords schönsten Gebäuden; von diesem Turm singt der Collegechor jedes Jahr am ersten Mai bei Sonnenaufgang. Auf dem 40 Hektar umfassenden Gelände findet man Uferwege, einen Wildpark und Gärten. Die Gebäude tragen besonders viele Wasserspeier, groteske Figuren.

Merton College   Merton Street   4F

Founded
1264 Walter de Merton.

Buildings
Chapel 1290; Bell Tower 1450. Mob Quad and Library 1304-78, Fellows' Quad 1610; St Alban's Quad 1910.

Past Members
John Wycliffe; Thomas Bodley; T.S. Eliot; Lord Randolph Churchill; Nevill Coghill; Kris Kristopherson.

Note
One of the three oldest colleges.
The chapel is the largest and the oldest in Oxford, and contains rare 13th-century stained glass. Library, in Mob Quad, is the oldest in England and contains examples of medieval books chained to the shelves

L'un des trois collèges les plus anciens d'Oxford.
La chapelle est la plus vaste et la plus ancienne d'Oxford, et l'on peut y admirer de rares vitraux du treizième siècle. La bibliothèque, située dans le Mob Quad, est la plus vieille d'Angleterre et renferme des exemplaires de livres médiévaux enchaînés aux étagères.

Eines der drei ältesten Colleges.
Die Kapelle ist die größte und älteste in Oxford und enthält seltene Glasmalereien aus dem 13 Jahrhundert. Im 'Mob Quad' befindet sich die älteste Bibliothek Englands. Sie enthält einige Exemplare mittelalterlicher Bücher, die zum Schutz vor Diebstahl angeketet wurden.

New College New College Lane & Holywell St 4E

Founded
1379 William of Wykeham, Bishop of Winchester.

Buildings
Great Quad, Chapel, Hall, 1380s; Cloister 1400. Garden Quad 1450-1718. Buildings on Holywell Street all 19th century.

Past Members
Bishop Henry Chichele (founder All Souls); Thomas White (founder Massachusetts); W.A. Spooner (Warden); Hugh Gaitskell; Tony Benn.

Note
Seventh oldest college. Founded as St Mary College of Winchester in Oxford, but called New College to distinguish it from Oriel.
W.A. Spooner, Warden 1903-24, had difficulty expressing himself, and unwittingly created the 'spoonerism'.

Septième collège établi. Fondé sous le nom de St Mary College de Winchester à Oxford, connu sous le nom de New College, pour le distinguer d'Oriel College. W.A. Spooner qui en fut le directeur 1903-1924 donna involontairement son nom au 'spoonerism' (contrepèterie).

Das siebtälteste College. Gegründet als St Mary College of Winchester in Oxford, aber New College genannt, um es von Oriel College zu unterscheiden. W.A. Spooner, Warden von 1903-1924, dem es zu Zeiten schwerfiel, die richtigen Worte zu finden, wurde, ohne es zu wollen, zum Begründer des 'Spoonerism'.

Oriel College Oriel Square   3E/F

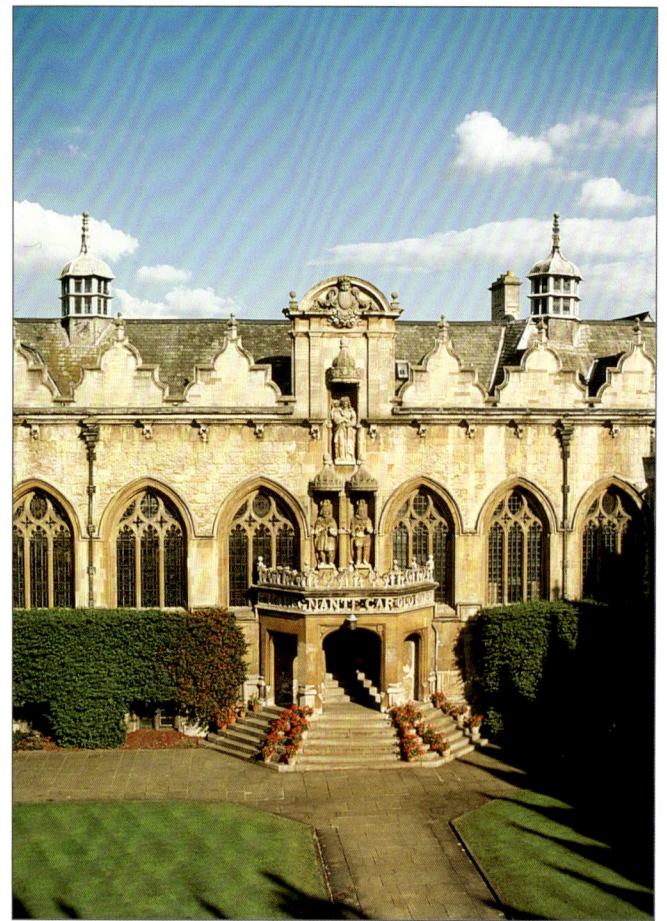

Cinquième collège établi à Oxford.

Berceau du 'Mouvement d'Oxford' qui se développa entre 1830 et 1840. Ce mouvement, conduit entre autres par Newman et Keble, visait à la réforme de l'Eglise Anglicane. Dernier collège d'hommes à adopter la mixité, en 1985 seulement, Oriel a une longue tradition d'excellence en matière de courses d'aviron, et acquiert progressivement la même réputation dans le domaine académique.

Das fünftälteste College. In den 30er und 40er Jahren des 19 Jahrunderts die Heimstätte des sog. Oxford Movements (einer kirchlichen Reformbewegung). Unter den Reformern u.a. Newman und Keble. Bis 1985 letztes reines Männercollege in Oxford. Oriel hat eine lange Erfolgsgeschichte im Rudern vorzuweisen und reüssiert nun auch zunehmend auf akademischem Gebiet.

Founded
1326 Adam de Brome, as 'The House of the Blessed Mary the Virgin in Oxford'.

Buildings
Front Quad 1620-40, Back Quad 18th century. Cecil Rhodes Building, 1911.

Past Members
Sir Walter Raleigh; John Keble; Cardinal Newman; Samuel Wilberforce (Bishop of Oxford); Cecil Rhodes.

Note
Fifth oldest college. Home of the Oxford Movement, 1830s-40s; Newman, Keble and others who would have reformed the Church of England. Last college to remain all male (until 1985) Oriel has a long tradition of eminence in rowing, and now increasingly in academic work.

Pembroke College   St Aldate's   2/3F

Founded
1624 Thomas Tesdale and Richard Wightwick, of Abingdon.

Buildings
Old Quad 17th century, Chapel Quad 19th; Chapel itself fine ornate Baroque 1732, Street front 1525, begun by Cardinal Wolsey.

Past Members
Samuel Johnson; James L. Smithson (the Smithsonian Institute); Patrick Campbell; Michael Heseltine.

Note
Named for the Earl of Pembroke, then Chancellor. Notable for having the rebellious and poor Samuel Johnson briefly as an undergraduate. A recent Master was Sir Roger Bannister, the first man to run a sub-four-minute mile.

Apelé ainsi en hommage au Comte de Pembroke qui fut Chancelier de l'Université. Connu aussi pour avoir eu brièvement parmi ses étudiants le pauvre et rebelle Samuel Johnson. L'un de ses directeurs fut Sir Roger Bannister, le premier homme à avoir parcouru un mille en moins de 4 minutes.

Bennant nach seinem Gründer dem Earl of Pembroke, der zur Zeit der Gründung Kanzler der Universität war. Der so rebellische wie arme Samuel Johnson studierte hier eine kurze Zeit lang. Ein vor kurzem Master war Sir Roger Bannister, der die Meile als erster unter vier Minuten lief.

The Queen's College High Street   4E

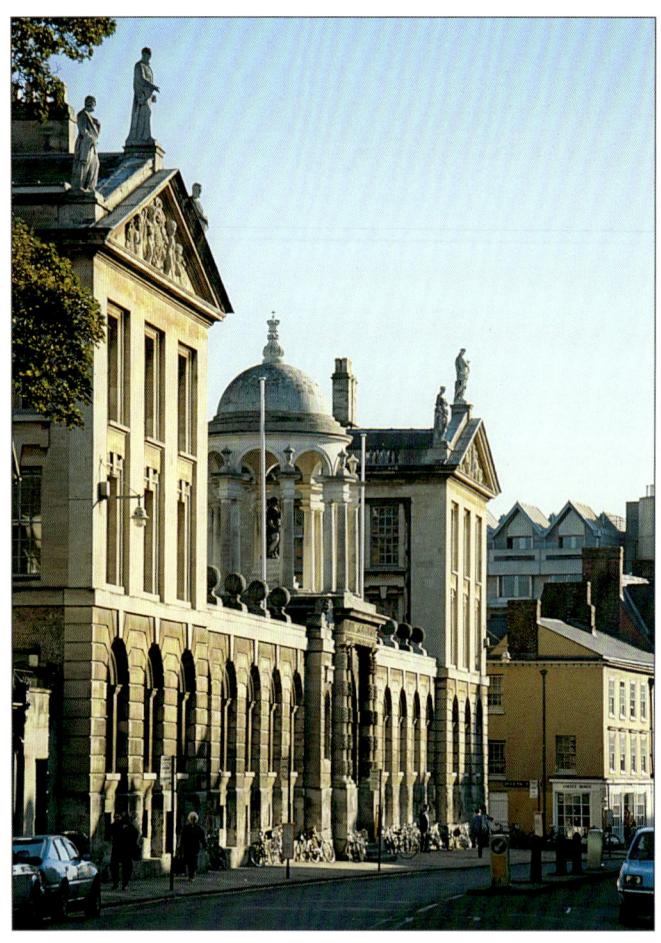

Sixième collège établi à Oxford.
Fondé à l'intention des étudiants du nord de l'Angleterre. Le Prinicpal et douze membres devaient se mettre à table selon les peintures de la Sainte Cène, selon les volontés du fondateur du collège. Dernier collège à avoir cessé de brasser sa propre bière.

Das sechstälteste College. Ursprünglich bestimmt für Gelehrte und Studenten aus Nordengland. Der Provost und zwölf Fellows waren aufgefordert, sich beim Abendessen so zu gruppieren, wie man es von Gemälden des letzten Abendmahls kannte.

Founded
1341 Robert de Eglesfield of Cumberland, Chaplain to Queen Philippa.

Buildings
High Street front and Front Quad, chapel and hall, early 18th century. North Quad, library 1695.

Past Members
Edmund Halley (astronomer); Howard (Lord) Florey (Provost); Brian Walden, Rowan Atkinson.

Note
Sixth oldest college. Intended for scholars from the north of England. The Provost and twelve Fellows were required to sit at dinner as in paintings of The Last Supper, as the founder laid down. Last college to cease brewing its own beer.

St Edmund Hall Queen's Lane 4E

Founded
1270 as Academic Hall, college status 1957.

Buildings
Front Quad, various periods, new quad 1970. Library in ancient church of St Peter, with crypt of about 1100.

Past Members
Oronhyatekha (Mohawk Chief); Sir Robin Day.

Note
Named for St Edmund Rich, who lived and taught here in the 1190s. One of Oxford's oldest academic houses, originally owned by Oseney Abbey. In 1557 it was bought by Queen's, who ran it until it acquired independent college status in 1957. Formerly a modest house, now one of the larger colleges.

Nommé ainsi à cause de St Edmund Rich qui habita et enseigna ici dans les années 1190. L'une des plus anciennes salles universitaires qui appartenait à l'origine à l'Abbaye de Oseney. Racheté en 1557 par Queen's College, qui le dirigea jusqu'à ce qu'il acquiert le statut de collège indépendant en 1957. Modeste demeure lors de sa fondation, il est aujourd'hui l'un des plus grands collèges d'Oxford.

Bennant nach St Edmund Rich, der gegen Ende des 12 Jahrhunderts hier lebte und lehrte. Eine von Oxfords ältesten akademischen Einrichtungen, ursprünglich im Besitz von Oseney Abbey. Das benachbarte Queen's College kaufte es im Jahre 1557, und unter seiner Leitung blieb es, bis es im Jahre 1957 Collegestatus erhielt. Früher ein bescheidenes Haus, heute eines der größeren Colleges.

St John's College St Giles   2D

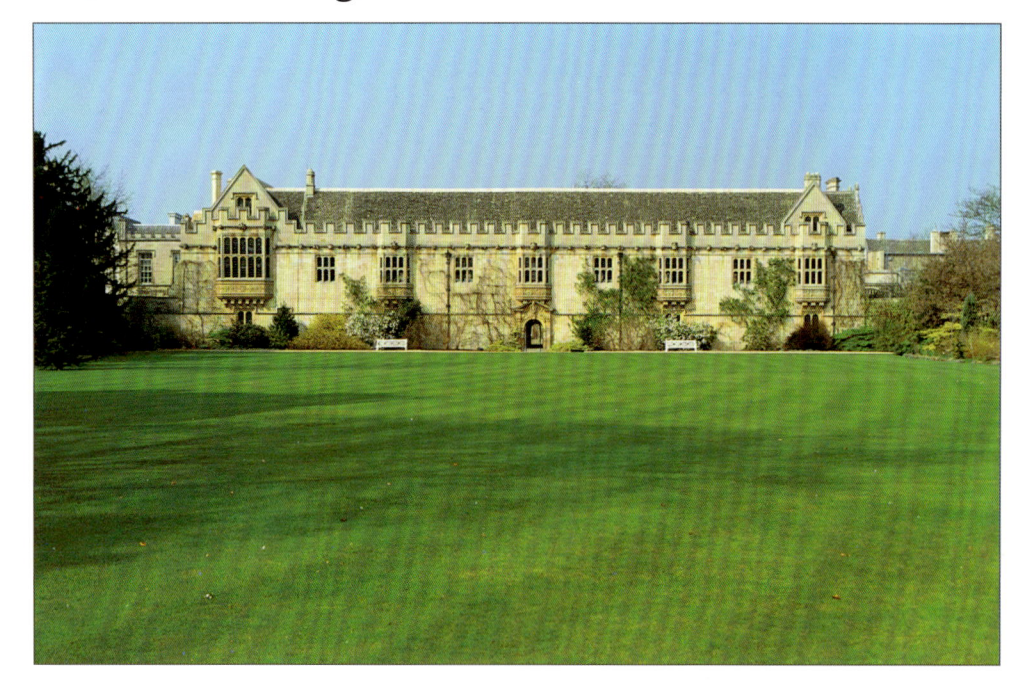

Founded
1555 Sir Thomas White, in former St Bernard's College, 1437, buildings.

Buildings
Front Quad late 1400s; Chapel and hall 1500s. Canterbury Quad 1636. Garden Quad.

Past Members
Edmund Campion (R C Martyr); William Laud; Kingsley Amis; L.B. Pearson (Canadian PM); Dean Rusk (USA); Tyrone Guthrie; Robert Graves; Philip Larkin.

Note
Founded by a Roman Catholic in the year the Protestant Bishops were martyred. Most famous son was William Laud, 1573-1645, scholar, Fellow 1593, and President 1611 of the college, Chancellor of the University 1629-40, Archbishop of Canterbury 1633.

Fondé par un catholique pendant l'année où les évêques protestants étaient martyrisés. Son plus célèbre *alumnus* fut William Laud, 1573-1645, étudiant, membre en 1593, président du collège en 1611, Chancelier de l'Université de 1629 à 1640, et enfin archevêque de Canterbury en 1633

Berühmtestes Collegemitglied war William Laud (1573-1645), der am College studierte, 1593 Fellow des Colleges und 1611 dessen Präsident wurde. Von 1629 bis 1640 Kanzler der Universität war er. 1633 ernannte man ihn zum Erzbischof von Canterbury.

Trinity College Broad Street 3D/E

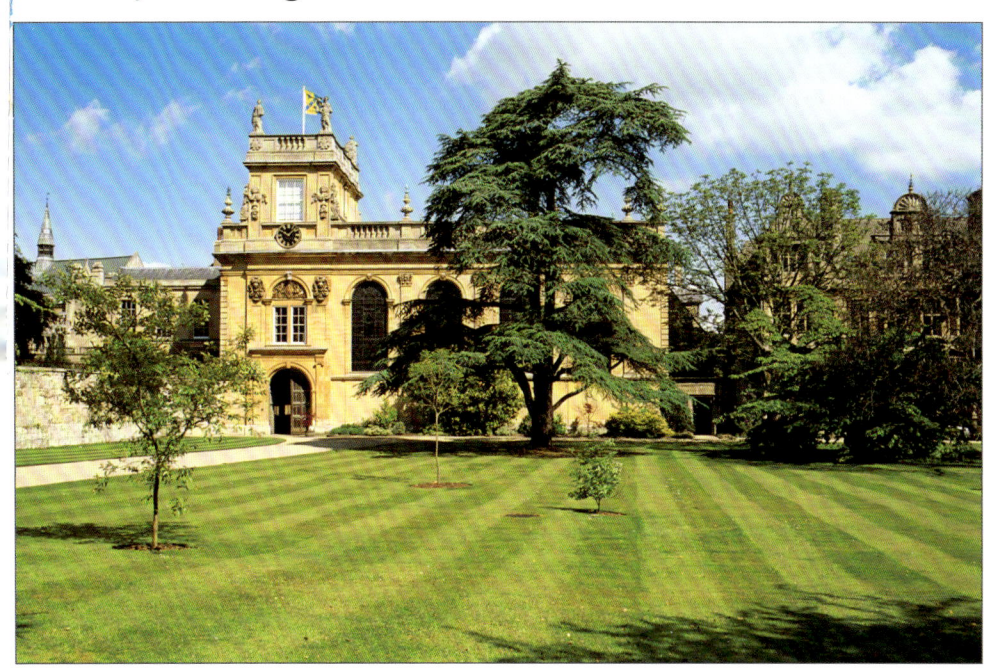

Founded
1555 Sir Thomas Pope on site of dissolved Durham College of 1286.

Buildings
Front Quad, garden-like; east range 1887 by Thomas Jackson. Chapel 1694 Dean Henry Aldrich, Durham Quad 1421. Garden Quad 1668 by Wren. Modern Cumberbatch Quad with Blackwell's Norrington Room below ground.

Past Members
Gilbert Sheldon (Archbp); Cardinal Newman; William Pitt the Elder; Jeremy Thorpe.

Note
The eccentric Ralph Kettell, President 1599-1643, carried scissors to use on scholars whose hair he thought too long. Trinity brewed the best beer in Oxford so that scholars should not be tempted into the town to 'comfort their stomachs'.

Ralph Kettell, Président de 1599 à 1643, avait coutume de porter sur lui des ciseaux afin de couper les cheveux des étudiants quand il les estimait trop longs. Trinity College brassait la meilleure bière d'Oxford, et évitait ainsi que les étudiants ne soient tentés d'aller 'réconforter leurs estomacs' hors des murs du collège.

Der exzentrische Ralph Kettell, Collegepräsident 1599-1643, trug immer eine Schere mit sich, um den Studenten ihm, deren Haare ihm zu lang erschienen, zu Liebe zu rücken. Trinity braute einst das beste Beir in Oxford, damit die Gelehrten nicht in Versuchung geführt würden, ihren Liebern in der Stadt Gutes zu tun.

University College   High Street   4E

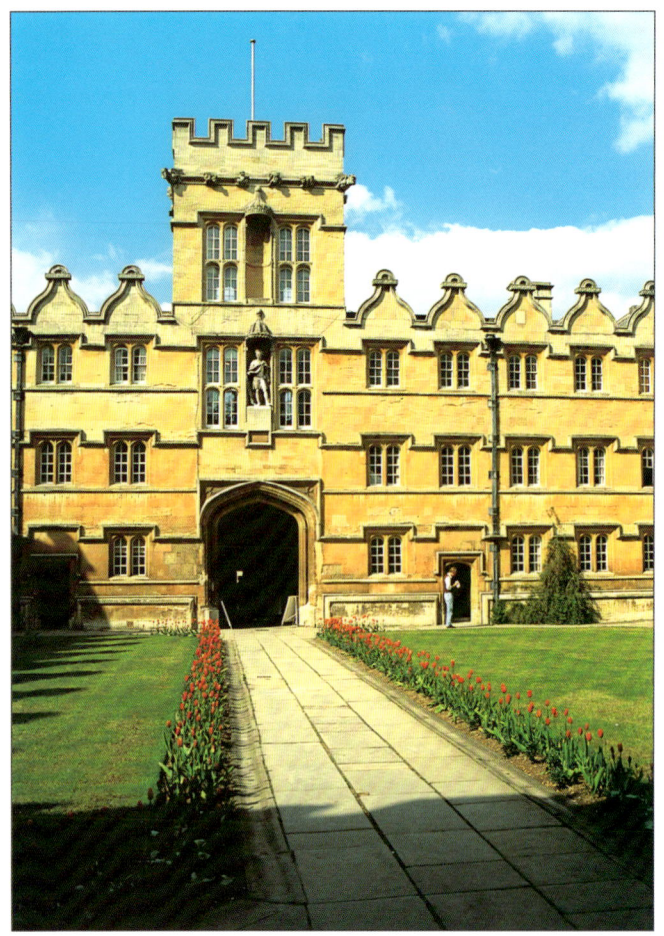

Founded
1249 William, Archdeacon of Durham.

Buildings
Front Quad 1634, chapel 1666; Radcliffe Quad 1717; Goodhart Building, 1962; Shelley Memorial 1894.

Past Members
Dr John Radcliffe; Percy Bysshe Shelley; C.S. Lewis; Clement Attlee; Harold Wilson (Fellow); Richard Ingrams; Bill Clinton.

Note
The oldest collegiate foundation. Did not have its fixed home on this site until the 1330s. The poet Shelley, 1792-1822 was briefly an undergraduate. He was a disorderly young man who conducted scientific experiments in his room and spoiled the furniture; he was expelled for writing a pamphlet in support of atheism.

Le collège le plus ancien d'Oxford.
Installé dans les bâtiments actuels à partir des années 1330. Le poète Shelley (1792-1822) y fit un bref passage estudiantin. Il fut un jeune homme désordonné qui conduisait des expériences scientifiques dans sa propre chambre et détruisait le mobilier. Il fut renvoyé pour avoir écrit un opuscule en faveur de l'athéisme.

Die älteste Collegegründung. Das College hatte bis in die 30er Jahre des 14 Jahrhunderts keine feste Heimstätte auf seinem jetzigen Gelände. Shelley (1792-1822), der berühmte romantische Dichter, studierte hier kurze Zeit, Der aufrührerische junge Mann führte auf seinem Zimmer wissenschaftliche Versuche durch und beschädigte das Mobiliar. Das College verwies ihn wegen einer Streitschrift, die den Atheismus unterstützte.

Wadham College Parks Road   3D

Founded
1610 Nicholas and Dorothy Wadham of Somerset.

Buildings
Central buildings 1610-13; Modern buildings in and adjoining King's Arms pub and houses in Holywell Street. Fine garden.

Past Members
John Wilkins (Warden); Christopher Wren; Thomas G. Jackson; Michael Foot; Melvyn Bragg.

Note
College built in only three years under the command of Nicholas Wadham's widow Dorothy, already in her seventies. John Wilkins, Warden 1648-59, with Christopher Wren and other scientists, founded the Royal Society in London.

Ce collège fut édifié en trois années seulement, à la demande de la veuve de Nicholas Wadham, Dorothy, alors qu'elle avait déjà plus de soixante-dix ans. John Wilkins, directeur de 1648 à 1659, ainsi que Christopher Wren et d'autres scientifiques, fondèrent la Société Royale, à Londres.

Unter der Aufsicht von Nicholas Wadhmas über siebzigjähriger Witwe Dorothy wurde das College in nur drei Jahren erbaut. John Wilkins, Warden von 1648 bis 1659, gründete zusammen mit Christopher Wren und anderen Wissenschaftlern die 'Royal Society' in London.

Worcester College   Worcester Street   1D/E

Founded
1714 Sir Thomas Cookes.

Buildings
Central buildings 1720s to 1780s (Hawksmoor and George Clarke); south side of quad 15th-century cottages. Modern additions. Spacious gardens, fine trees, famous lake.

Past Members
Rupert Murdoch; John Sainsbury; Richard Adams.

Note
The medieval cottages are a rare survival from the Benedictine Gloucester College of 1283. The classical main buildings are good examples of 18th-century pomposity. The park and lake offer a romantic setting for drama productions on summer evenings.

Les cottages médiévaux sont une survivance du Bénédictin Gloucester College de 1283. Les bâtiments principaux de style classique sont un bon exemple du dix-huitième pompeux. Le parc et le lac constituent une mise en scène romantique naturelle pour les soirées théâtrales.

Die mittlalterlichen Cottages sind ein ungewöhnlicher Überrest von Gloucester College, einer 1283 gegründeten Klosterschule der Benediktiner. Die klassizistischen Hauptgebäude sind schöne Beispiele für den prunkvollen Stil des 18.Jahrhunderts.

Other Colleges

Keble College

Green Templeton College -1979 & 1995. The two colleges merged in 2007. Woodstock Road - map ref 1B
Set up in and around the 18th-century Radcliffe Observatory. Graduate-only college, with a focus on a range of subjects generally concerned with human welfare.

Keble College - 1868 - Parks Road - map ref 3C
Founded, with public subscription, by the Oxford Movement in memory of the leader John Keble.

Kellogg College -1990 (as Rewley House) - Banbury Road Map ref 2A
One of Oxford's largest and most international graduate colleges.

Linacre College - 1962 - St Cross Road - map ref 4C
Provides a college life for visiting graduates.

Lady Margaret Hall-1878-Norham Gardens-map ref 3A Set up by Dame Elizabeth Wordsworth and friends to promote university education for women.

Mansfield College - 1830 - Mansfield Road - map ref 3D
Nonconformist theological college, now open to all students.

Harris-Manchester College - 1997 - Mansfield Road - map ref 4D
A 19th-century foundation for nonconformists, now a fully federated college in the University.

Nuffield College - 1937 - New Road - map ref 1/2E
Founded by W.R. Morris (Lord Nuffield), the motor magnate, to promote studies in industry.

St Anne's College - 1879 - Woodstock Road - map ref 2B
Founded to promote the university education of women.

St Antony's College - 1948 - Woodstock Road - map ref 2B
Specialises in studies of other regions.

St Catherine's College - 1942- Manor Road-map ref 5D
Set up in 1868 as a house for non-collegiate students.

St Hilda's College - 1893 - Cowley Place-map ref 5G
Founded to promote the education of women in Oxford.

Other Colleges, Buildings and Museums

St Hugh's College - 1866 - St Margaret's Road-map ref 1/2A
A second foundation for women by Dame Elizabeth Wordsworth.

St Peter's College -1929-New Inn Hall Street- map ref 2E
Founded Revd Christopher Chavasse as a hall for 'Low-Church' men of modest means; independent college status since 1961.

Somerville College - 1879 - Woodstock Road - map ref 2C
Set up for the university education of women and named after the scientist Mary Somerville (1780-1872).

Wolfson College - 1966 - Linton Road (N. Oxford)
Provides college life for unattached graduates and their families. Modern riverside buildings.

St Cross College - 1966 - St Giles - map ref 2D
Established to provide a house for non-college lecturers and graduates. Originally in an old school building near St Cross church, it is now at Pusey House, St Giles.

OTHER BUILDINGS

Carfax Tower - 1200s - map ref 2/3E Ancient belfry; visitors may climb to the roof.

Oxford Castle - 1070 - New Road - map ref 1F
Now redeveloped as a premier visitor attraction.

Martyrs' Memorial - 1843 - St Giles - map ref 2D
To three Protestant Bishops burned at the stake, 1555-6.

St Michael at the North Gate - AD 1000 - Cornmarket - map ref 2E
Tower is the oldest building in Oxford; museum and shop.

MUSEUMS

Old Ashmolean - Broad Street - map ref 3E
Scientific Equipment

Ashmolean - Beaumont Street - map ref 3F
Art Gallery

Christ Church Gallery - map ref 3F
Art Gallery

Faculty of Music -St Aldates map ref 3G
Musical Instruments (Bate Collection)

Museum of Modern Art - map ref 2F
Contemporary Work

Above: Somerville College
Opposite: The Radcliffe Camera

Oxford Life

Above all rivers the Cherwell is idyllic for punting - the leisurely poling along of a comfortable flat boat.
On the Thames (or Isis) the more energetic sport of rowing: the river is too narrow for side-by-side racing, so the aim is to 'bump' the boat in front.
Most sports are practised at Oxford, some with matches against Cambridge; outstanding performers are rewarded with a 'Blue', and may become famous. Life is not all study and exertion: there are the colleges' Commemoration Balls in the summer, Bump Suppers for rowing successes, Gaudy Nights, and other merry-makings.
There are solemn ceremonials: *Encaenia* for conferring honorary degrees on prominent people and for delivering dull orations; regular degree-giving; the University Sermon at St Mary's Church every Sunday.
For different entertainment there is the Oxford University Dramatic Society, OUDS, which has launched many famous actors.
Countless music societies and several choirs provide frequent concerts.
For aspiring politicians and barristers the Oxford Union Society offers parliamentary style debating and a bit of notoriety.

Parmi toutes les rivières qui traversent Oxford, le Cherwell est idéal pour la pratique du 'punting', qui consiste à faire avancer, avec mesure, un long bateau à fond plat à l'aide d'une perche.
Sur la Tamise, on pratique un sport plus énergique: l'aviron. Mais la rivière étant trop étroite pour des courses de front, il s'agit de talonner le bateau de tête.
La plupart des sports sont pratiqués à Oxford et de vigoureuses compétitions sont organisées avec Cambridge. Les sportifs les plus remarquables sont récompensés d'un 'blue'.
Mais la vie à Oxford n'est pas qu'étude et exercice physique: il y a aussi les bals commémoratifs des collèges pendant l'été, les 'Bump Suppers' pour fêter les victoires à l'aviron, les 'Gaudy Nights' et beaucoup d'autres réjouissances. Il y a aussi les cérémonies solennelles: *Encaenia* pour remettre les diplômes *honoris causa* aux personnalités éminentes et qui est l'occasion d'assommants discours; aussi le sermon dominical à l'église St Mary.
Toutes sortes de spectacles sont organisés par l'association dramatique d'Oxford (OUDS), qui a lancé de nombreux acteurs anglais. Des associations musicales et plusieurs choeurs confèrent à Oxford une vie musicale active.
Pour les aspirants politiciens et avocats, l'Oxford Union Society offre des débats 'comme à l'assemblée' qui permettent à la fois de s'exercer à ces professions et d'acquérir quelque notoriété..

Mehr als alle anderen Flüsse eignet sich der idyllische Cherwell zum 'Punten', zum gemächlichen Dahintreiben im flachen Kahn - als Steuer und Antrieb dient eine Stange.
Auf der Themse (oder Isis) dagegen geht es energischer zu: es wird gerudert. Der Fluß ist zu schmal für herkömmliche Rennen, Ziel ist es deshalb, das vordere Boot 'anzustoßen'.
Man treibt die unterschiedlichsten Sportarten in Oxford, einige haben ihre regelmäßige Wettkämpfe gegen Cambridge. Wer sich besonders hervortut, erhält ein 'Blue', und so mancher wurde schon berühmt.
Das Leben besteht nicht nur aus Studium und Anstrengung. Im Sommer finden die Collegebälle statt, die Ruderer feiern ihren Erfolg mit ausgiebigen Gelagen, Ehemalige treffen sich zu besonderen Festlichkeiten u.v.a.
Doch gibt es auch würdevollernste Zeremonien: Die *Encaenia*, anläßlich deren man bedeutende Persönlichkeiten mit akademischen Graden ehrenhalber ausstattet und einfallslose Reden hält. Die reguläre Verleihung akademischer Würden. Die Universitätspredigt in der St Mary's Kirche.
Viele Musikgesellschaften und Chöre geben Konzerte.
Politikern und Anwälten in spe bietet die renommierte Oxford Union Society Debatten in parlamentarischem Stil.

Parks

University Parks - Parks Road. A park since the 17th-century or earlier; now well planted with fine trees, some exotic. Bordered on one side by the Cherwell; on the other side, the University Cricket Ground.

Botanic Garden - High Street. Combines botanical research with pleasure; a wealth of fine trees and foreign plants and entrancing glass houses.

Christ Church Meadow - St Aldate's, Rose lane. A large pastoral meadow of 20 hectares bounded on two sides by the rivers Thames and Cherwell; a highly valued open space in the centre of the city.

South Park - Headington Hill. A little beyond St Clement's towards Headington; a spacious park partly on high ground with fine views of the city.

Port Meadow - Walton Well Road, Aristotle Lane. Said to be England's oldest and largest continuous meadow; it has belonged to the city of Oxford for at least 900 years. It covers some 160 hectares (400 acres) and may be used only for grazing and recreation. It is bordered on one side by the Thames.

University Parks - Ce parc a été planté dans la forme qu'on lui connait aujourd'hui au dix-septième siècle et peut-être même avant. Il compte des arbres magnifiques et de nombreuses essences rares. Il est bordé d'un côté par la rivière Cherwell. De l'autre côté, se trouve le terrain de cricket de l'université.

Botanic Garden - Il joint les recherches botaniques au parc d'agrément. Abondance de beaux arbres et de plantes des pays lointains. Les serres sont magnifiques.

Christ Church Meadow - Est une grande prairie pastorale d'une vingtaine d'hectares, bordée sur deux côtés par la Tamise et la Cherwell. C'est véritablement un très bel espace vierge au centre de la ville.

South Park - Situé peu après St Clement, sur la route de Headington: vaste parc, en partie planté sur une colline, d'où l'on a une très belle vue sur la cité.

Port Meadow - On dit qu'elle est la plus ancienne et la plus grande prairie d'Angleterre. Elle appartient à la cité d'Oxford depuis plus de 900 ans. Elle couvre 160 hectares (400 acres), et ne peut être utilisée que pour le pâturage et pour les loisirs. Elle est bordée d'un côté par la Tamise.

University Parks - Der Park besteht mindestens seit dem 17. Jahrhundert. Er ist mit sehr schönen, zum Teil exotischen Bäumen bepflanzt. Auf der einen Seite grenzt er an den Cherwell. Auf der anderen Seite des Parks liegt das Kricketgelände der Universität.

Botanic Garden - Hier lassen sich botanische Forschung und Erholung verbinden. Viele wunderschöne Bäume und fremdländische Pflanzen sowie eindrucksvolle Gewächshäuser.

Christ Church Meadow - Ein 20 Hektar großer Weidegrund, auf zwei Seiten von der Themse bzw. dem Flüßchen Cherwell eingefaßt. Willkommenes Freigelände mitten in der Stadt.

South Park - Jenseits St Clement's Road und Richtung Headington gelegen, ein weiträumiger, zum Teil ansteigender Park mit sehr schönen Ausblicken auf die Stadt.

Port Meadow - Angeblich Englands ältester und größter Weidegrund. Gehört seit mindestens 900 Jahren zu Oxford und umfaßt ein Gebiet von 160 Hektar. Genutzt werden darf dieses Gelände nur zur Erholung und um Vieh zu weiden. Auf einer Seite wird es durch die Themse begrenzt.